Your Environment

Wildlife IN DANGER

Jen Green

Franklin Watts
London • Sydney

How to use this book

This series has been developed for group use in the classroom, as well as for students reading on their own. Its differentiated text allows students of mixed reading abilities to enjoy reading and talking about the same topic.

① The main text and ② picture captions give essential information in short, simple sentences. They are set in the © Sassoon font as recommended by the National Literacy Strategy document *Writing in the Early Years*. This font style helps students bridge the gap between their reading and writing skills.

③ Below each picture caption is a subtext that explains the pictures in greater detail, using more complicated sentence structures and vocabulary.

④ Text backgrounds are cream or a soft yellow to reduce the text/background contrast to support students with visual processing difficulties or other special needs.

Saving animals

We can protect rare ①
species by creating
nature reserves.
A nature reserve can be a
home for many animals.

⇧ **Tourists with manatees** ②

Nowadays many people visit ③
reserves to see wild plants and
animals in natural settings. ④

© Aladdin Books Ltd 2004

Designed and produced by
Aladdin Books Ltd
2/3 Fitzroy Mews
London W1T 6DF

First published in
Great Britain in 2004 by
Franklin Watts
96 Leonard Street
London EC2A 4XD

ISBN 0 7496 5502 X

A catalogue record for this book is available from the British Library.

Printed in UAE

Editor:
Jim Pipe

Educational Consultant:
Jackie Holderness

Wildlife Consultant:
Helen Freeston

Design:
Simon Morse
Flick, Book Design and Graphics

Picture Research:
Brian Hunter Smart

CONTENTS

Introduction 4

Living together 6

Disappearing homes 8

Too many people? 10

Farming 12

Fishing 14

Pollution 16

Changing climate 18

Hunting 20

Pets and zoos 22

Unwanted visitors 24

Saving animal homes 26

Helping wildlife in danger 28

Wildlife project 30

Glossary 31

Index 32

Introduction

Many of us have a favourite wild animal, such as a tiger or bear.

But did you know that many wild animals and plants are now rare? Some may soon die out.

People are causing this problem. We hunt animals and destroy wild places.

Luckily, some groups are working to save rare plants and animals. We can all help.

▷ **Bison and many butterflies are rarer than they used to be.**

Extinct animals and plants are ones that have died out altogether. Wildlife that is very rare is called endangered.
   Endangered animals may be large like a bison, or small creatures like a butterfly. Hunters almost wiped out the bison. Many butterflies are threatened by global warming as well as by people destroying the wild places where they live.

⬇ **Dinosaurs died out long ago.**

A species is a particular type of plant or animal, such as the American bison. Extinction is when all the animal or plants of one type die out, so that none are left.

In the past, many species have died out, often because they couldn't cope with natural changes. The dinosaurs probably died out after a meteorite struck Earth and made conditions change very quickly. Now global warming is making conditions change quickly, too.

Living together

Living things are found almost everywhere on Earth – from the bottom of the ocean to the tallest mountain.

Every plant and animal lives in a particular kind of place. This is its habitat. Over time, wildlife slowly changes to suit its habitat.

Plants and animals in one habitat depend on each other. If any die out, others suffer.

◁ **Living things in a habitat depend on each other for food.**

The plants and animals in a habitat are connected in a food chain. If one link in the chain is removed, other creatures suffer. ① Plants make their own food using sunlight energy. ② Animals such as deer, rabbits and insects eat plants. ③ Hunters such as owls, cats and foxes eat other animals. ④ When living things die their remains nourish the soil, so that more plants can grow.

▷ **Bees help plants. They carry pollen between flowers.**

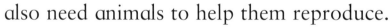

Animals depend on plant food, but many plants also need animals to help them reproduce.

Bees carry pollen from one flower to another. The pollen fertilises the plants so they can make seeds, which will grow into new plants. Without bees, the plants would die out too.

◁ **This deer is suited to life in a forest.**

Many plants and animals living in a habitat such as a forest have features that help with life there.

For example, this deer has a spotted coat that helps it blend in with the shady forest. Other types of deer that live in deserts or the Arctic have different-coloured coats to help them blend in.

▽ **These iguanas live only in the Galapagos Islands.**

Some types of animals are found in different habitats and in many parts of the world. For example, red foxes can live in forests, grasslands and deserts.

Other plants and animals are only found in just one small place, where they are suited to particular conditions. For example, marine iguanas live only in the Galapagos Islands which lie 1,000 kilometres off the coast of South America.

Disappearing homes

All over the world, plants and animals are in trouble. This is mainly due to people taking over the wild places where they live.

Most plants and animals are suited to one particular place.

They cannot just go somewhere else. Also, there are few wild places left for them to go.

⬆ **People have cut down the forest home of this Tamarin monkey.**

⬆ **Draining marshes threatens animals like this damselfly.**

Rivers, lakes and ponds are home to ducks, fish, frogs, otters and insects.
When people drain these wetlands to make way for fields and towns, they threaten all these animals. The Norfolk damselfly from England died out because people drained the wetlands where it lived.

Tropical rainforests are home to millions of different types of plants and animals. Scientists believe over half of all land species live there.
However, huge areas of forest have now been cut down for fuel or timber, or to clear the land for farming. Forest animals such as the Golden Tamarin have less and less room to live in.

▽ Mining disturbs Arctic animals such as reindeer.

The snowy wastes of the Arctic are home to animals such as polar bears and reindeer. Beavers and bears live in the dense forests to the south.

Few people live in these remote areas, but in some places, mining for gold or oil is harming the environment. The construction of pipelines to carry oil across the Arctic disturbs wild reindeer, called caribou.

▽ Wildlife cannot thrive in tiny pockets of woodland like this.

In some places, whole forests have been cut down, leaving just a small patch. These tiny, isolated habitats are too small for forest plants and animals to thrive.

People can help by planting trees to link small woodlands. Animals can then use these leafy corridors to move from one wood to the next.

Too many people?

Around the world, the number of people is growing.

We live in almost every corner of Earth, except for icy wastes and mountains.

People are taking over more and more wild land. Plants and animals have less and less space to live in.

⬇ **Tourists disturb turtles nesting on beaches.**

Turtles spend their lives at sea, but come ashore to lay their eggs on beaches. The bright lights of new hotels on nesting beaches confuse the adult turtles and also the babies that hatch out from the eggs.

⬆ **Animals such as this badger die on busy roads.**

As human numbers rise, villages spring up on wild land and slowly grow into towns. Roads linking towns cut though forests and grasslands.

Many animals are run over on busy roads. During the 1990s, one in five badgers in the Netherlands were killed every year on the country's roads.

⇧ **Each year, there are more and more people on Earth.**

Two hundred years ago, there were one billion (one thousand million) people on Earth. Now there are over six billion.

Forests are cut down and other wild places are taken over just to provide the space we need to live in. Wild places where animals and plants can live are getting smaller and smaller.

⇩ **A few animals, such as raccoons, are at home in towns and cities.**

As towns and cities expand, so most wild animals are driven out. However, a few kinds of animals have adjusted to city life.

Frogs, squirrels, butterflies and birds make homes in gardens and parks. Foxes, rats and raccoons search for food among our rubbish.

Even in cities it is important to keep areas of woodland and marsh that can provide a home to rare species such as otters and voles.

Farming

As human numbers grow, more and more wild land is used to grow crops and raise animals.

Today, many farmers also use chemicals to grow bumper crops. These harm wild creatures.

Fields that were once home to all kinds of wildlife now hold just one crop.

⬆ **Prairie chickens almost died out due to habitat loss in the US.**

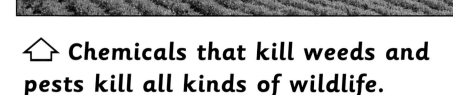

⬆ **Chemicals that kill weeds and pests kill all kinds of wildlife.**

Many farmers spray their crops with chemicals to get rid of weeds and insects. These poisons kill all kinds of wildlife. However, organic farmers grow crops without using chemicals. Many more species are found on their farms.

Wild grasslands such as the American prairies once covered large areas on many continents. Now much of this wild land has been ploughed up to grow crops. This has almost caused some wild birds such as prairie chickens to die out.

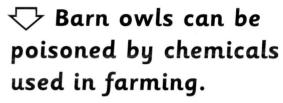

Goats have eaten all the grass on this farm in Africa.

Farmers rear herds of cattle, sheep and goats on land that is too poor for crops. But sometimes domestic animals strip all the vegetation, so wild creatures have nothing to eat.

If all the grass is eaten, winds and storms can blow or wash away the soil. This problem is called erosion.

Barn owls can be poisoned by chemicals used in farming.

When farmers spray their fields to get rid of pests, wild animals are affected too. The poison can spread through the food chain.

Mice absorb the chemicals when they eat grain that has been sprayed. The poison is stored in their bodies. Barn owls that eat poisoned mice may die, too.

Fishing

The oceans cover over two-thirds of Earth's surface. They provide a habitat for fish, whales, seals, crabs and many other animals.

Fish are an important food for people worldwide.

However, modern fishing boats catch so much that now fish are scarce in many seas.

▷ **Puffins go hungry when fish are scarce.**

Whales, seals and seabirds such as puffins depend on fish. When fish are scarce, these hunters go hungry and cannot raise their young.

Many countries now set limits on the amount of fish their fleets can catch. This allows the fish to recover. Some fishermen also use nets with larger holes that allow young fish to escape.

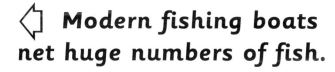

Modern fishing boats net huge numbers of fish.

People have always gone fishing, but in past times, fishing methods weren't so effective. Nets were also smaller, so fewer fish were caught.

Now fishing fleets use huge nets to catch fish. In some places there are not enough fish left to breed. These seas have been "overfished".

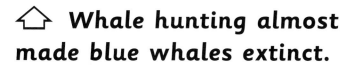

Whale hunting almost made blue whales extinct.

Whales were once hunted for their meat and also for oil to light lamps. About 50 years ago, so many whales had been killed that many species were in danger of dying out.

People realised the danger and very few countries still hunt whales. But many species are still endangered.

Dolphins sometimes drown in fishing nets.

Dolphins are sometimes caught in the nets of fishermen hunting tuna and other fish. They are no use to the fishermen, so they are just thrown back to rot.

Some fishermen use nets with special safety hatches that allow dolphins to escape. But these nets still kill dolphins, while long lines kill seabirds such as albatrosses. All tuna species are now endangered because of overfishing.

Pollution

Pollution is dirtying the air, water and land with waste that people don't want. Pollution threatens wildlife all over the world.

Homes, farms, factories and power stations all give off waste. It drifts in the air, seeps through the soil or spreads in rivers, lakes and oceans.

◁ **Thousands of reindeer died after the nuclear accident at Chernobyl.**

Many countries have strict laws to prevent pollution. But accidents still cause pollution.

In 1986, the nuclear power plant at Chernobyl in Russia let off a cloud of radiation. The cloud drifted on the wind, poisoning lichen and other vegetation in northern Europe. Reindeer that fed on the lichen were poisoned and had to be killed.

△ **Acid rain has wiped out fish in many lakes.**

Factories, power stations and cars give off waste gases as they burn fuel such as coal and oil. The gases mix with water vapour in clouds to make a weak acid, which later falls as acid rain.

The acid kills trees and plants, and drains off into rivers to harm fish, frogs and snails. In Canada, over 30,000 lakes have been damaged by acid rain.

▽ Litter can kill wildlife like this seagull.

Pollution includes litter that people drop carelessly. Broken glass, rusty tins and plastic can cut, choke or poison wild animals.

Plastic bags left on the beach drift out to sea, where sea turtles mistake them for jellyfish and swallow them. The animals die of suffocation. So always take your litter home with you.

◁ This seal is covered in oil spilled by a tanker.

Oil spills at sea cause pollution. The sticky, black oil spreads over the water surface. It clogs the feathers and fur of birds and mammals, which get sick and die.

In 1989, the oil tanker *Exxon Valdez* was wrecked off the coast of Alaska. A huge oil slick polluted 2,000 kilometres of coastline. Half a million seabirds and 5,000 sea otters died.

Changing climate

Factories, power stations and cars give off waste gases. These pollute the atmosphere.

This pollution is trapping the Sun's heat near the Earth. This is helping to make the weather warmer.

This is called "global warming". It is already causing problems for wildlife in many parts of the world.

▷ **Global warming threatens coral reefs rich in sea life.**

Coral reefs are living communities of sea creatures called polyps. These reefs provide a home for fish and many other creatures. However, coral polyps can only thrive in clear, shallow water of a certain temperature.

Warmer water, rising sea levels and pollution are all harming the coral, causing a threat to other reef life.

Global warming is melting the polar ice. This threatens penguins.

As temperatures rise, the ice in the polar regions is beginning to melt. This threatens the survival of polar animals such as seals, penguins and polar bears.

The melting ice is making sea levels rise. Whole islands may one day disappear beneath the waves, wiping out local wildlife.

Climate change may have wiped out the Golden Toad.

Global warming is causing swamps and pools to dry out in many areas. This threatens amphibians such as the European natterjack toad.

In Central America, scientists report that the Golden Toad has already died out, probably due to warming in its forest habitat.

We can all help to reduce the damage caused by global warming.

We all add to the problem of global warming as we travel in cars and planes that give off waste gases, and use energy produced by power stations. So everyone can help to reduce the effects of global warming.

Switching off machines when you're not using them helps to save energy. Walking, cycling or using public transport causes less pollution than going by car.

Hunting

For thousands of years, people have hunted animals for meat and for their skins.

People once hunted with simple weapons. But modern weapons make killing easy. Hunters may soon wipe out some animals.

Some people hunt animals for sport. We also kill sharks and tigers because they frighten us.

▷ **People kill cheetahs for their beautiful fur.**

Around the world, many kinds of animals are still hunted for their skins and other body parts. Big cats such as cheetahs are killed for their fur, which is used to make expensive clothes.

Elephants and rhinos are hunted for their tusks and horns, which are used to make ornaments. A lot of this killing is now against the law, but it still goes on.

◁ Chimpanzees are now rare because of hunting.

Hundreds of years ago, people lived by hunting wild animals and gathering plant food. Now farms and ranches provide the food we need, but in some countries, hunting still goes on.

In Africa, rainforest animals are hunted and sold as "bushmeat". Threatened species include gorillas and leopards.

⬆ Farmers set traps for foxes that steal chickens and lambs.

Dangerous creatures such as tigers, sharks and poisonous snakes are hunted because people are frightened of them.

Farmers set traps for foxes and wolves because they sometimes kill farm livestock. All kinds of other animals die in the traps.

⬇ Passenger pigeons died out because of sport hunting.

Hunting also goes on in the name of sport. In the space of just a few centuries, European hunters wiped out a bird called the passenger pigeon in North America.

Passenger pigeons were once found in huge numbers, but their large flocks made easy targets for European hunters. The very last passenger pigeon died in a zoo in 1914.

Pets and zoos

Some animals and plants are rare because people take them from the wild and sell them.

People who steal rare animals and plants are called poachers. Most poached animals become pets. Others end up in zoos.

In the past, zoos treated animals badly. But many zoos today are helping to save rare species.

 **Some poachers steal young apes.**

Poaching for the pet trade threatens apes such as orang-utans, as well as small creatures like reptiles, fish and even spiders.

The poachers usually kill the adult apes and steal their babies because they are small and easier to manage. Many baby apes also die because their new owners don't look after them properly.

⬆ **People capture parrots for sale as pets.**

Most animals taken from the wild do not thrive away from home. Captured animals are frightened and confused. Many are sold abroad. On the journey they are often kept in cramped cages. Many die on the way.

Ninety types of parrot are endangered because so many birds have been captured as pets.

▽ Animals born in the wild do not usually make good pets.

If your family buys a pet, make sure that is has been bred from captive animals, not taken from the wild. The pet shop should tell you where the animal came from.

Parrots, reptiles, fish and other animals bred in captivity make better pets than wild ones, because they are more used to humans and easier to look after. Make sure you find out about the food and conditions your pet needs.

◁ Many zoos today are trying to save rare species like condors.

In the past, animals in zoos were not always well treated. Some were kept in small cages. A few species almost died out because too many were captured for zoos.

Nowadays, zoos often help to save rare species, by breeding the animals in captivity. If breeding is successful, the young animals may be released into the wild.

23

Unwanted visitors

When people bring new species into a habitat, they can threaten local plants and animals.

The new plants and animals can also cause big changes in their new habitat.

Plant-eaters take the food of local animals, while new hunters kill local wildlife.

⬆ **Rabbits brought to Australia nibble pastures bare.**

⬆ **People brought mongooses to hunt rats, but they became pests.**

People have brought new animal hunters to many areas. Mongooses were introduced to Puerto Rico to hunt rats. But they soon threatened local snakes and spread the disease rabies to other animals on the island.

New wildlife brought to Australia caused great changes there. Some of the newcomers took over from local species.

European settlers released rabbits in Australia. The new arrivals bred quickly and became pests, stripping grasslands bare. This left no food for local species. Rabbits are now killed as pests.

Water hyacinth is now a pest on many waterways.

New plants as well as animals can become pests when they thrive in their new homes.

In the 19th century, a pretty plant called the water hyacinth from South America was released in lakes and ponds in North America, Africa and Asia. It spread quickly and now completely chokes waterways in many areas.

Hedgehogs brought to the Hebrides steal birds' eggs.

Animals of remote islands are particularly threatened by new predators because they are often not used to being hunted.

On the lonely Hebrides Islands in Scotland, local seabirds are threatened by hedgehogs. These were brought to the islands to eat snails and slugs in people's gardens, but they now prey on birds' eggs.

Scientists are trying to reduce the number of hedgehogs on the islands. But there is a lot of disagreement between bird lovers and hedgehog lovers.

Saving animal homes

All over the world, wildlife groups are working to save rare wildlife. This is called conservation.

Creating nature reserves helps to protect rare species. This saves whole areas of habitat.

People also need to take better care of nature everywhere. We should live in ways that don't harm wildlife.

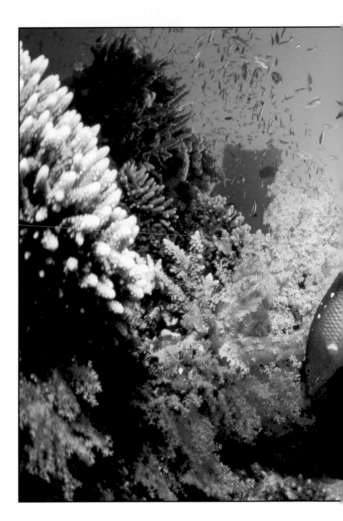

▷ **Tourists visit reserves to see rare animals such as these manatees.**

⬆ **This coral reef is in a nature reserve.**

Many people visit reserves to see wild plants and animals in natural settings. The visitors pay a fee which helps to pay for conservation work in the park. This is called eco-tourism.

Reserves also provide jobs and money for local people. Rare mammals called manatees are protected in reserves on US coasts.

In many parts of the world, reserves and national parks now protect wild areas. Building and mining is banned in these areas, and no one is allowed to pick plants or harm wild animals.

Marine reserves are just as important as parks on land. The Great Barrier Reef in Australia is a protected coral reef.

Endangered animals sometimes have to be moved to places of safety, called sanctuaries, for their own protection. In New Zealand, the introduction of cats and other predators brought the flightless Takahe to the edge of extinction.

Conservationists took some of the last birds and released them on a tiny island offshore, which was first made safe from predators. Cats, weasels, and rats were removed to make the island safe.

◁ **Ladders help salmon to swim upriver to lay their eggs.**

Many animals make yearly journeys to safe places where they can breed. Fish such as salmon, birds and whales all make these regular journeys, called migrations. Salmon swim upriver to breed. If dams block their way, the fish cannot breed successfully.

Many dams now have ladders. A ladder is a series of steps and pools, one above the other, that help the salmon to swim upriver.

Helping wildlife in danger

We must do more to protect nature. Without our help thousands of species may die out in the next fifty years or so.

Loss of wild habitats, global warming and pollution are all big problems in many places.

People all over the world are now working hard to save rare species. But it can only work if we all help.

▷ **Conservation groups help to save rare species such as whales.**

Campaign groups such as the WWF (World Wide Fund for Nature) have helped to save many rare species. Greenpeace helped to convince many countries to ban whaling, in order to save whales from extinction.

Everyone can help with conservation work by joining a wildlife organisation. You could take part in a sponsored walk to raise money for your favourite animal.

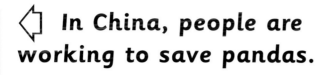

◁ **In China, people are working to save pandas.**

In China, giant pandas are in danger of dying out because of loss of their forest habitat. Only 1,000 of these animals remain.

Twelve forest reserves have been set up to save pandas in the wild. Zoos have also managed to breed baby pandas from captive animals. Captive breeding projects like this are very expensive, so they can only help to save a few species.

◁ **A ban on hunting protects this beautiful butterfly.**

In the 1970s, many governments signed an agreement called the Convention on International Trade in Endangered Species (CITES).

CITES bans trade in most wild animals including this birdwing butterfly. Sadly the profits that can be made from wildlife are big and many people ignore the law.

▽ **These children are learning about rare species in their area.**

If you want to find out more about endangered wildlife, try these websites:

- UK Wildlife Trusts
  www.wildlifetrusts.org
- WWF (World Wide Fund for Nature)
  www.worldwildlife.org
  www.panda.org/kids
- International Union for Conservation of Nature & Natural Resources:
  www.iucn-uk.org
- Environment Australia On-line
  www.deh.gov.au
- US Fish and Wildlife Service
  www.endangered.fws.gov/kids/ how_help.htm
- Friends of the Earth
  www.foei.org
- Department of Conservation, New Zealand
  www.doc.govt.nz/index.html

Wildlife project

Joining a conservation group can help to save wildlife all over the world. Wildlife in your local area may also be in danger of dying out.

You could also write a letter to your **MP** or local council. Tell them your worries about local wildlife.

The first step is to find out about the wildlife in trouble.

plant

snail

frog

heron

◁ 1. Find out about the wildlife in your area.

Find out as much as you can about plants and animals in a wild place near you, such as a woodland, pond, heath, or local nature reserve. Identify the species you see using a book about local wildlife.

Binoculars can help you to spot distant animals, while a magnifying glass can be useful for small creatures. Always take a trusted adult with you to keep you safe.

2. Draw a food chain linking the plants and animals you have seen.

Use books or the internet to find out more about the habits of local creatures. Do the animals you saw eat plants, or do they hunt other creatures for food? Draw a diagram to show how local plants and animals are linked in a food chain. For example, snails feed on water plants. Snails are eaten by frogs, who in turn are eaten by herons.

3. Join in with work to help local wildlife.

Find out if any of the plants and animals you have seen are scarce. If so, do you know why? Wildlife books and the internet will have details. Find out what is being done to help local wildlife. Can you join in? For example, you could help to clear litter from local streams or woodlands.

GLOSSARY

Captivity – When an animal is kept in a confined space, such as a cage.

Conservation – Work that is done to protect wildlife.

Endangered – Of a plant or animal species that is very rare, and in danger of dying out.

Extinct – When a type of plant or animal dies out completely, so that none of that species are left alive.

Global warming – The increased warming of weather worldwide, caused by air pollution.

Habitat – A particular place where plants and animals live, such as a rainforest.

Organic farming – A type of farming in which farmers do not use chemicals such as pesticides.

Overfishing – When so many fish are caught that not enough are left to breed, so that the total number of fish drops.

Pesticides – Chemicals used by farmers/gardeners to kill weeds and animal pests that harm their crops.

Species – A unique type of plant or animal, such as the African elephant.

INDEX

acid rain 16

birds 11
  condors 23
  owls 6, 13
  parrots 22, 23
  Passenger pigeons 21
  penguins 19
  prairie chickens 12
  puffins 14
  Takahe 27

captivity 23, 31
chemicals 12, 13
conservation 26-27, 28-29, 30, 31
coral reefs 18, 26

dinosaurs 5

endangered 4, 31
extinct 4, 5, 12, 21, 31

fish 8, 14-15, 18, 23
  salmon 27
  tuna 15

food chain 6, 13, 31
frogs 8, 11

global warming 5, 18, 31
Golden toad 19

habitats 6-7, 8, 31
hunting 4, 6, 20-21

insects 6
  bees 7
  butterflies 4, 29
  damselfly 8

mammals
  American bison 4, 5
  badgers 10
  cheetas 20
  chimpanzees 21
  deer 6, 7
  dolphins 15
  foxes 6, 7, 11, 21
  goats 13
  Golden Tamarin 8
  hedgehogs 25
  manatees 26

mongooses 24
orang-utans 22
otters 8, 11
pandas 29
polar bears 9, 19
rabbits 6, 24
raccoons 11
reindeer 9, 16
whales 15

oil spills 17
organic farming 12, 31
overfishing 15, 31

pests 12, 13, 24, 25
pets 22-23
pollution 16-17, 18

reptiles
  marine iguanas 7
  turtles 10, 17

species 5, 31

websites 29

zoos 22-23

Photocredits
Abbreviations: l-left, r-right, b-bottom, t-top, c-centre, m-middle
Front cover tl — Select Pictures. Front cover c, 15ml — Dr. Louis M. Herman/NOAA. Front cover bl & br, back cover tr, 18tr, 20br, 22bl — Digital Stock. Back cover tl, 1, 2mr, 3mr, 6bl, 19tr, 26c, 28tr — Photodisc. 3tr, 6tl, 14bm, 23ml, 26-27t, 29ml, 30mr — Stockbyte. 3br, 19ml — Charles H. Smith/U.S. Fish & Wildlife Service. 4br, 30tr — Otto Rogge Photography. 4-5 — Jack Dykinga/USDA. 6mlt — Ken Hammond/USDA. 6mlb — John Foxx Images. 6br, 7tr, 8ml, 10mr, 10-11t, 13bl, 20tr, 24tr, 30mtb — Corel. 7mt — Corbis Royalty Free. 8tr — PBD. 9bl, 16-17t, 17ml, 27ml, 29ml, 30bl — U.S. Fish & Wildlife Service. 9br — Argentinian Embassy, London. 10bl — NOAA. 11br — Dave Menke/U.S. Fish & Wildlife Service. 12ml — John Deere. 12-13t — George Lavendowski/U.S. Fish & Wildlife Service. 13tr, 21ml, 28br — Corbis. 14r — Jose Cort/NOAA. 15tr — Tom Kieckhefer/NOAA. 16ml — Captain Budd Christman/NOAA Corp. 17br — P. Martinkovic/U.S. Fish & Wildlife Service. 18br — Florida Keys Marine Sanctuary. 21tr — Luther Goldman/U.S. Fish & Wildlife Service. 22-23t — John & Karen Hollingsworth/U.S. Fish & Wildlife Service. 23br — Comstock. 24bl — Gary M. Stolz/U.S. Fish & Wildlife Service. 25bl — Ted Center/USDA. 25tr — Jim Pipe. 27br — Peter LaTourrette. 30mtt, 31ml — Sherry James/U.S. Fish & Wildlife Service.